THE ANIMALS' ARRIVAL

THE ANIMALS'
ARRIVAL

Elizabeth
Jennings

DUFOUR
1969

Dufour Editions, Inc
Chester Springs, Pa. 19425

Library of Congress Catalog Card Number 69-19124

PRINTED IN GREAT BRITAIN BY
NORTHUMBERLAND PRESS LIMITED
GATESHEAD

For Peter Levi

CONTENTS

THE ANIMALS' ARRIVAL

So they came
Grubbing, rooting, barking, sniffing,
Feeling for cold stars, for stone, for some hiding-place,
Loosed at last from heredity, able to eat
From any tree or from ground, merely mildly themselves,
And every movement was quick, was purposeful, was proposed.
The galaxies gazed on, drawing in their distances.
The beasts breathed out warm on the air.

No-one had come to make anything of this,
To move it, name it, shape it a symbol;
The huge creatures were their own depth, the hills
Lived lofty there, wanting no climber.
Murmur of birds came, rumble of underground beasts
And the otter swam deftly over the broad river.

There was silence too.
Plants grew in it, it wove itself, it spread, it enveloped
The evening as day-calls died and the universe hushed, hushed.
A last bird flew, a first beast swam
And prey on prey
Released each other
(Nobody hunted at all):
They slept for the waiting day.

THE DAY

I get up shaken by all my nightmares,
the day is grey and pushes itself against
my windows. 'Greyness', I say, 'come in,
you have after all merged with magnificent night
and know its contours and stars.' Here there is nothing
but a few awkward objects. I have to salute them
and learn them again and even perhaps love them.
The lunar mysteries seem so far away
and the sun is also hidden. Someone below
is shaking a carpet, someone is clipping the lawn,
Good labours these, and behind the many windows
men are sporting with what their minds contain,
making them almost computers. Noises are what
this world is really mapped with, the scrape on a scythe,
a man whistling, a bird pecking for food,
a carpet-sweeper next door. Down the lane are coming
taxis and lorries. Next door a very old woman
opens the door and smiles at remaining flowers.
Something is plucking her too, beyond the daybreak.
I am my senses letting the day come in.

SCULPTOR

Not his hands but his face, watch,
It opens suddenly, suddenly,
He knows that something will happen
And with the most gentle touch
And a fierce inward cry
He waits for the clay to open.

Then he is most eloquent,
Hands move, depart, return,
Slowly a statue appears.
Against his clay he is a faint
Force, yet he can make it burn
Like a hundred blazing fires.

He is different with bronze,
Must build up, build up.
The final cast will show
How much he had to arrange.
His hands will fall back, drop,
Only now he begins to know.

A PATTERN

A pattern will emerge, is emerging,
Not simply the embroidered sky showing

What we could never do, but in ourselves,
In our thoughts even, there evolves

A strange mystery and the clue to it,
Pick up the images, let them fit.

And let the astounding earth reveal its creatures,
Each with its own peculiar features.

I am, standing here watching, watching
And if I move, everything is touching me, is touching.

FIRST MAN

There must be language found for this —
The first man prodding without emphasis,

For soft ground, a warm home,
A kind of living, a rhythm.

Behind him is all
The past painted on a wall —

Intrepid deer, unusual birds
And everything, everything without need of words.

There is a sudden halting. The man has found
Need for a god in the forefront of his mind.

He appears, O the daring and beauty,
This suddenly needed deity.

And man kneels
Knowing that this god heals.

The spreading tree holds the harsh fruit
That will call man and sear him to the root.

A SIMPLE SICKNESS

Sickness so simple that a child could bear it
And bear it better. There would be so much —
The soldiers flung among the pillows: dolls
Brought to abrupt confusion down the bed,
And violent Chanticleer, *his* voice gone hoarse,
Crowing quite soundlessly at all the farm —
A child would have all this and know it too.

I only have my grown-up troubles now
And grown-up, half-dead words to speak them in.
Illness for me has no true absolute
Since so much of my daily action is
Dressed up in pain. Why am I lying here,
Voice gone, lips dry, chest fiery, mind quite wild
Begging the past back, longing to be a child?

THE PLOUGH

Plough there and put your seed in deeply.
The sky wants it and our eyes too.
Look how gently moon shows you to us,
But there is heaving, deep working there.

I watch you from a telescope,
I hold you for an instant
Then I must run to the world of images.
Speculation is gone. It is we who are human
Who named that happy arrangement of stars
The plough and suggested the planting of seeds?

FIRE

It is a wild animal,
It is curling round objects,
It is greasy with candles,
And they run trickling down the walls
Making tributaries.
It is as if bad weather were perpetual.

And we found it
Only just in time.
We threw wet rags on the flames
Flung the books out,
Stamped on the sparks.
At last it was over
And we looked at the dead objects.

Not still-lives any more but still-deaths.
Ruin comes so easily and reminds us
We too might have been destroyed;
I picked up a loved book but was dumb to tears.

And today I am numb still
Shocked to silence and lost
From such little tragedy.
Big ones build in the mind;
We are so near to paper
To nothingness
So, in the power of nature
I shall not light candles again for a long time.

OF LANGUAGES

That time is approaching just
When the old imperious request
Can be forgotten in an hour of lust:

When the climates of terror retire
And leave only an aching fear
And the huge longing not to be here.

If I were painting I would put
A head down and hands — the paint still wet —
And eyes pleading something to forget.

As it is, with only a dry word
I seek yeast for my own bread
Yet find that it has, unnoticed, stirred.

That hour is approaching now
When the language must be sudden and new
And the images sharp, still, slow.

THE SOLDIERS

Sometime they will come.
Maybe upon an easy August day.
They will come swaggering into a room,
Loosen their belts and say,
'We are not what we seem.'

The way that they behave is quite at odds
With all their easy speeches.
Something in this invasion is like the gods
Or like a man who preaches,
Catching up all the congregation's moods.

I woke this morning early, could not hear
The noise of soldiers moving round the house.
Silence was simple: it was everywhere
Enclosing us.
And yet within the distance the taut drums
Were trembling for the fingers' throb and stir.

THE UNKNOWN CHILD

That child will never lie in me, and you
Will never be its father. Mirrors must
Replace the real image, make it true
So that the gentle love-making we do
Has powerful passions and a parents' trust.

That child will never lie in me and make
Our loving careful. We must kiss and touch
Quietly, watch our own reflexions break
As in a pool that is disturbed. Oh take
My watchful love; there must not be too much.

A child lies within my mind. I see
The eyes, the hands. I see you also there,
I see you waiting with an honest care,
Within my mind, within me bodily,
And birth and death close to us constantly.

NEVER TO SEE

Never to see another evening now
With that quick openness, that sense of peace
That, any moment, childhood could allow.

Never to see the spring and smell the trees
Alone, with nothing asking to come in
And shake the mind, and break the hour of ease —

All this has gone since childhood began
To go and took with it those tears, that rage.
We can forget them now that we are men.

But what will comfort us in our old age?
The feeling little, or the thinking back
To when our hearts were their own privilege?

It will be nothing quiet, but the wreck
Of all we did not do will fill our lack
As the clocks hurry and we turn a page.

RESOLVE

So many times I wrote (before I knew
The truth of them) of horror and of fear;
The words came easily, each phrase seemed true,
And yet there was a polar atmosphere,
A coldness at the heart. I knew it too.

Now that I have lived in the midst of pain
And madness, and myself have gone half mad,
I shall not make the same mistake again
Or write so glibly of the sick, the sad.
I want Equators in my writing, rain
Warm from the Tropics, pungent, quick and sane.

BIRTH

That was a satisfaction of the sense —
That country where no reason reigned at all.
We heard the cries, we saw the apple fall.
This was how every animal begins.

I could put out my hand and touch the source
Of life; intensest pleasure filled my blood.
And then the waking-up: what conscience could
Restrain, it stopped. The throbbing water-course

Was damned, the sense of drowning played a drum
Deep in my ears, then silence and I came
Like children to a country I could name
Because one trusted voice had whispered 'Come'.

HOSPITAL GARDEN

This is the first time I have been alone
For one whole month. Summer is really here
And silence too. Yes, you could drop a stone
Into the hazy, humming atmosphere.

They will return — the nurse, the patients too
And I must write down this before they come.
My inward needs and fears still stir and grow
Into a hideous and a nightmare form.

I am not drugged as all the others are.
My naked senses, totally awake,
Respond at once to pleasure and endure
Immediate pain. I know that I must make

My life again. Yes, make myself as well.
(I hear a ringing in the distance stop)
Now for a second I am out of hell
And Limbo too. The screams, the voices drop.

But only for an instant is there peace.
Someone is walking swiftly down the lawn.
Was it a dream that I felt quite at ease?
In the stark day all answers are withdrawn.

INTERVIEWS

(FOR S.S.)

'You hate him', 'No, you love him', so they say,
Simply because I meet him every week
And talk. We are a doctor, patient and
Know well the various terms on which we speak.

I thought I hated him, but I was wrong;
I found that out one day when he, in pain,
Bore two hours' suffering while I talked on.
I shall not make the same mistake again.

What then is generated by these speeches?
Compassion, pity, envy? None of these.
It is because we know no rock-bare beaches
That we can anchor, fitfully at ease.

THE SOURCE

It was as if I went back to the source
Of life. I smelt the things, the strings of birth—
Milk, grass, a stable and a water-course,
And always the rank stench of fertile earth.

Primeval slime found stirring on a rock —
That is how life and history were viewed
By our great-grandfathers. I say a shock,
A flash of nerves, a glimpse of something nude —

All these are nearer to the truth, but still
Something is unexplained. Why should we fear
To love as deeply as we dread to kill?
I do not know. Too many dreams crowd near.

THE BROKEN MINDS

These broken minds of which I too am one
Have no power now to shake my faith at all,
I do not ask: What has this person done
That they should have such punishment?; The Fall
Explains it all.

But many question how the Fall took place
Or wonder if it is a fancy built
By man to save his reason and his face
And exorcise the sharp, fierce sense of guilt
Of which we are built.

The madness here increases every day;
The screams invade each room, each corridor.
Dreams overlap my waking in a way
That troubles and confuses me much more
Than when the corridor

Is paved with vomit and with broken glass.
Terror has many forms: it can appear
Gently like shadows which discreetly pass
Or as an all embracing atmosphere,
The very absolute of fear.

COLD WINTER

I wait and watch. The distances disperse,
Snow is stored up within the lowering sky.
Only still life would seem to spill and lie
Waiting for someone to observe it there,
Stand for a moment, warm behind thin glass.

Chatter of birds, cars in the distance hum
Yet everything seems moving in my head.
This is the silent season when the dead
Slip from their bodies in a cold dark room,
What once was life is memory instead.

And yet one shift of snow, one shaft of light
And all I know of spring comes back to me.
It is as if my arms could be a tree,
Bearing and blossoming within the night
And then at daylight struggling to be free.

LOVING

Loving, I return
Years back into a time
Where only the young burn
While the old ones rhyme.

I have thought too much
Of this thing and of that.
I become out of touch
And everything seems flat:

Is it? Or do I
Change what I half-perceive,
Half-look, so falsify
And keep up my sleeve

Mask, tricks and children's games.
(I know the tricks of some)
Yet with my passions, dreams,
I am silent, struck dumb.

HUNTING

All night long they are hunting in the dark,
The doctors, patients, nurses, children, and birds.
Some are flying in actual forests and some
Are merely moving in conversation or dreams.

But all are searching, all have weapons or traps,
Most have become quite expert at their sport.
For some it is not a sport but life itself —
For the birds, I mean, and perhaps the children too.

What will they do when they finally run it down,
Stare in the steady, gleeful eyes of the foe?
Will the ropes, the stones, the shot, the bullets, the words,
The dangerous dreams, be enough for its overthrow?

AGO

Old.
Few years more attend me, I am redundant
A useless tool, a broken body, seedless.
Look at me and you see a season regretting.

I foresaw this once
But it was not like this. I saw
An age of goodness, of gifts spent out and needed.
Age is a going back.

Is a kind of return,
To the breast, the womb, the mother.
I do without all and face the winter regretting.
The child in me who can play no longer.

WAKING

I have woken out of this cunning sleep;
Beasts — heraldic — formed my memories.
My nightmares were masters. No servant tended them
But they demanded my coherence and clear acceptance.
I am awake, awake among crumpled sheets.

The beasts in my mind, the acts will not leave me,
A moment ago I was running
Down green lawns to a sheer cliff,
I stopped with my feet on the edge of the grass
And behind, behind

One nameless pursued me, went over the cliff,
And wingless flew to a certain death.
Meanwhile my fingers turned on the sheets.
I was coming alive, I was coming to.
The nightmares were ending.

So we make globes and so they are visited.
In the shape of the skull, the lobes of the brain;
Worlds are forming on numerous pillows,
And what if we met each other within them —
What cliffs there would be, what deaths, what encounters!

BONNARD

Colour of rooms. Pastel shades. Crowds. Torsos at ease in
brilliant baths. And always, everywhere the light.

This is a way of creating the world again, of seeing differences,
of piling shadow on shadow, of showing up distances, of bringing
close, bringing close.

A way of furnishing too, of making yourself feel at home — and
others. Pink, flame, coral, yellow, magenta — extreme colours
for ordinary situations. This is a way to make a new world.

Then watch it. Let the colours dry, let the carpets collect a
little dust. Let the walls peel gently, and people come, innocent,
nude, eager for bed or bath.

They look newmade too, these bodies, newborn and innocent.
Their flesh-tints fit the bright walls and floors and they take
a bath as if entering the first stream, the first fountain.

24

MATADOR

He will come out with grace and music.
Watch his clothes fit him,
How he struts before you,
Now he is proud, proud.

No matter what happens,
Whatever blood is shed,
There will always be elegance;
This is what we have come for,
This is his *raison d'être*.

Oh I am thrilled by the excited air,
By the trumpets, the voices.
We are near to death here yet strangely, strangely,
It is life we celebrate.
We vaunt and taunt the rainbow spectacle,
Olé, olé, olé.

SAND

It is falling through my hand,
It is stretching along beaches,
The tide draws and drags it
But look, look,
I have caught it in my fingers.
I am holding the tides.

But wait, wait,
There is order here also.
The glass holds the sand,
The sand holds the sea.
At night the moon intervenes
But it cannot break my glass.

Only I can do that
But I am holding the sea at a distance.

THIS SUMMER

It is endless — this summer.
Roses topple over and their petals
Strew the lawn, scar the turf.
Wasps are beginning to swarm.

And at night we feel
All the heats subdued under the stars.
Flies batter against lampshades,
Moths make huge shadows.

And in our sleeps (O enter them, enter them)
There are strange losses and searches,
A feverish hunting, an unquiet pulse,
Then the warm morning suddenly waiting.

THE SEA

It is over there, far out.
It comes at us in hints, in salt and sounds
Or a few birds playing carry it
As the dove carried the olive-branch.
It is calm, calm from here.
We are safe inland.

But if we move toward the beach
A thousand shells will ring out the music of distance,
Shingle will slide, sand be fingered.
It is all, all there.

You can watch it for ever.
It is the symbol of variety,
Never, never the same,
And if you enter it and let the waves cover you
A spectrum of colour appears.
This is a science of seeing.

Anything can be likened to it, birth, death, love,
Most of all love.
Those breakers carry pure sound and pleasure,
Then they recede to gentleness.
But the sea is never subdued.

DEMANDS

Perhaps I ask
That life shall always
Excite, enchant.
I do not want
Drab, calm days,
The facile task.

Yet what I have
Now, this hour
Is still, is smooth,
Days pass with
Ease I deplore.
And so with love —

It has become
A matter of
Patience, waiting
And I am getting
A kind of love
I did not dream

Quite possible.
Absence has made
This mood, and you,
Withdrawn into
A different need,
Have made me feel

And learn also
That love in dead,
Dark times can grow.

LODGINGS

It isn't my house; only part of it
Contains a few of my own possessions —
A shadow flitting across the window,
An owl at night tending my ears,
And the books and papers I brought in with me.
I have no roots here. I do not fit.

And when I am lonely, loneliness is
Worse than at home, it brings all dreads,
Everything suddenly seems unfamiliar,
Even a letter I may be writing,
Even the doorbell ringing for me,
And the light on that opposite unfolding tree.

THE NIGHTMARES

They are coming slowly, slowly.
No act of faith is needed to credit them.
They inhabit your skull.

They inhabit your skull and people it,
People it not with shadows but with sharp light:
Your best moments are perverted.
You wake — sweating.

And turning, turning, you cry in a way children never do
Nor wild men.
There is a sad sophistication in it.
There is too much knowledge.
You stretch and reach to corruption.

OUTSIDE

Out there the darkness,
Here warmth, stillness,
Out there, frozen to still life
The world halts.
Inside the fire imitates the sun.
All South is there.
Outside no barometer,
No measurement for ship or bird,
No compass.

We move and fall in love
But our love is careful.
It has to be shielded
As you shield the flame of a lamp,
But it is entrance,
And central also
The great silence
The long nights.
Touching is always a caress, a warming.
Some lonely planet must be like this also.
I could not contend with it.

SILENCE OF WINTER

It grips hands, feet, whole body,
It reaches the heart by a quick route,
It makes portraits of faces, rearranging features
And always, always is quiet.

Soft, let the footsteps sink in the snow,
Let the voices disappear into whispers;
Think of the animals huddling in hibernation,
Of birds making small spurts for a crumb,
Of children hidden in mufflers.

It seems forever — this;
It seems as if fires will burn for ever,
As if logs will tumble to ashes,
Far off ships look for shelter and signals
And men are alive on their decks.

TRANSFIGURATIONS

The words will have to come without much ease —
Difficulty of tongue, an aching hand.
Sometimes they will not come at all, I know,
Merely belong to birds and far-off seas.
I shall be silent standing on the cliff.

And gulls will come and seem like symbols then.
I must know they are no such things, I must
Thrust them to their rock ledge once again
And hear the sea uninterrupted, coming
White, without words but meaning messages.

And I must learn a kind of morse, a signal,
Think of long strings being plucked, of the wheel turning
Bringing the pot to life. I shall need my fingers
But still not heed my older languages.
Hush for the silence in between the trees.

One word, perhaps, will come after this silence,
After this stillness; I must cherish it
And think how all the swooping of the gulls,
The sea, the cliff-top moved towards this end
And learn also how stars possess a pulse.

A LETTER TO PETER LEVI

Reading your poems I am aware
Of translucencies, of birds hovering
Over estuaries, of glass being spun for huge domes.
I remember a walk when you showed me
A tablet to Burton who took his own life.
You seem close to fragility yet have
A steel-like strength. You help junkies,
You understand their language,
You show them the stars and soothe them.
You take near-suicides and talk to them,
You are on the strong side of life, yet also the brittle,
I think of blown glass sometimes but reject the simile.
Yet about your demeanour there is something frail,
The strength is within, won from simple things
Like swimming and walking.
Your pale face is like an ikon, yet
Any moment, any hour, you break to exuberance,
And then it is our world which is fragile:
You toss it like a juggler.

THESE SILENCES

And they are there always, these silences:
Between drum and flute they utter their echoes,
Between voice and voice intervene with a laugh,
I have considered sometimes how one might catch them
As a note in music, a pause in feeling.
We are passionate men but need these intervals,
Our children break them with their first cry.

In each other's arms, lovers achieve them,
A haunting, a hunting, they are sure.
Beasts lurk in the long wait, or pursue their resting place.
Moments of peace are allowed like this.
I have felt them at night under many stars,
Under many truces, after all passion.

Once in the desert a man dragged himself
Far to oasis, his clothes gone to ribbons,
At first he wept with dry lips calling,
Then parched, as forever, gripped the sand in his fingers.
Water was scraped. Oh, water is silence
Or at least its likeness. He quenched his thirst.

CONGO NUN RAPED

This man tore open what I fiercely closed
Ten years ago. I do not hate him though
I lie here bleeding, cruelly exposed.

I chose cold weather just ten years ago
And he brought heat and sweat and nightmares too.
Why was I quick to him? I had been slow.

His seed is in me and a child may grow
Within nine months. I weep my vows away.
Fear fills me, all the statues seem to sway.

O God of love, what is it that I know?

MOTOR-RACER

It contains your intelligence,
The wheels spin, the gears hold,
Nothing is by chance.

From a distance one might
Suppose oneself on another planet
Or at the centre of the night.

Love, desire, all our human wants
Are in the movement, the sliding over oil.
Also in every distance.

Think yourself there, the perfect control
With the road spinning out for you
And with the whole

Globe, it seems, waiting for you to take over.
You watch, watch, then suddenly pounce
Either as enemy or as lover.

MEDITERRANEAN

Yes it is hard to believe
There are no tides, and yet
Its many moods convey
Sometimes a sense
Of a lithe suppleness
That always falls back to
Exactly the same place.

To this sea edge the sun
Is moon and draws along
Our helpless flesh and minds.

Our minds grow small, and bodies
Stretch to complete themselves.
They need this kind of sun,
Bold eyes and genitals
Ready to fling themselves
At once into embraces.
Yet everyone's apart
However much they cling.
The storm the sun demands
Is in the single heart.

ANY POET'S EPITAPH

It does this, I suppose — protects
From the rough message, coarseness, grief,
From the sigh we would rather not hear too much,
And from our own brief gentleness too.

Poetry — builder, engraver, destroyer,
We invoke you because like us
You are the user of words; the beasts
But build, mate, destroy, and at last
Lie down to old age or simply sleep.

Coins, counters, Towers of Babel,
Mad words spoken in sickness too —
All are considered, refined, transformed,
On a crumpled page or a wakeful mind,
And stored and given back — and true.